0509156

Masters of Music
THE WORLD'S GREATEST COMPOSERS

The Life and Times of

Hector Berlioz

Mitchell Lane
PUBLISHERS

P.O. Box 196
Hockessin, Delaware 19707

Masters of Music
THE WORLD'S GREATEST COMPOSERS

Titles in the Series

The Life and Times of...

Johann Sebastian Bach
Ludwig van Beethoven
Irving Berlin
Hector Berlioz
Leonard Bernstein
Johannes Brahms
Frederic Chopin
Duke Ellington
Stephen Foster
George Gershwin
William Gilbert and Arthur Sullivan
George Frideric Handel
Franz Joseph Haydn
Scott Joplin
Franz Liszt
Felix Mendelssohn
Wolfgang Amadeus Mozart
Franz Peter Schubert
John Philip Sousa
Igor Stravinsky
Peter Ilyich Tchaikovsky
Giuseppe Verdi
Antonio Lucio Vivaldi
Richard Wagner

Visit us on the web: www.mitchelllane.com
Comments? email us: mitchelllane@mitchelllane.com

Masters of Music
THE WORLD'S GREATEST COMPOSERS

The Life and Times of
Hector Berlioz

by Jim Whiting

Mitchell Lane
PUBLISHERS

Copyright © 2005 by Mitchell Lane Publishers, Inc. All rights reserved. No part of this book may be reproduced without written permission from the publisher. Printed and bound in the United States of America.

Printing   1   2   3   4   5   6   7   8
        Library of Congress Cataloging-in-Publication Data
Whiting, Jim, 1943-
        The life and times of Hector Berlioz / Jim Whiting.
            p. cm. — (Masters of music. The world's greatest composers)
        Includes bibliographical references (p.   ) and index.
        ISBN 1-58415-259-1 (library bound)
            1. Berlioz, Hector, 1803-1869—Juvenile literature. 2. Composers—France—Biography—
Juvenile literature. [1. Berlioz, Hector, 1803-1869. 2. Composers.] I. Title. II. Masters of music.
World's greatest composers.
ML3930 .B45W45 2004
780'.92—dc22
                                                                        2003024129

ABOUT THE AUTHOR: Jim Whiting has been a journalist, writer, editor, and photographer for more than 20 years. In addition to a lengthy stint as publisher of *Northwest Runner* magazine, Mr. Whiting has contributed articles to the *Seattle Times*, *Conde Nast Traveler*, *Newsday*, and *Saturday Evening Post*. He has edited more than 100 Mitchell Lane titles in the Real-Life Reader Biography series and Unlocking the Secrets of Science. A great lover of classical music, he has written many books for young adults, including *The Life and Times of Irving Berlin* and *The Life and Times of Frédéric Chopin* (Mitchell Lane). He lives in Washington state with his wife and two teenage sons.

PHOTO CREDITS: Cover, pp. 6, 21, 32, 35—Hulton Archive; pp. 1, 3, 9, 12, 18, 24, 26, 29, 38—Corbis; p. 16—Musée Hector Berlioz

PUBLISHER'S NOTE: This story is based on the author's extensive research, which he believes to be accurate. Documentation of such research is contained on page 47.

The internet sites referenced herein were active as of the publication date. Due to the fleeting nature of some web sites, we cannot guarantee they will all be active when you are reading this book.

Contents

The Life and Times of

Hector Berlioz

by Jim Whiting

* For Your Information

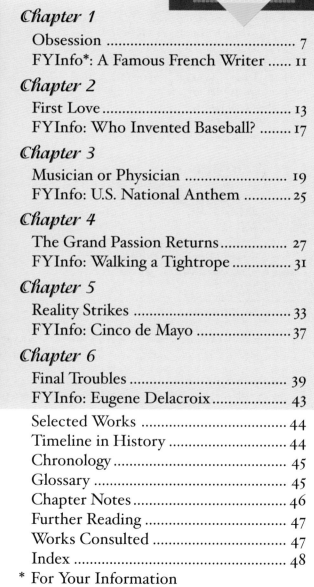

This photo of Hector Berlioz was taken in 1860, when he was 56. His pained expression may come from several physical ailments, which began bothering him about this time. Also, his greatest successes were far behind him.

Obsession

E arly in the 19th century, a young Frenchman saw a beautiful young woman. She had all the qualities that he was looking for in a wife. It was a case of love at first sight. His love became an obsession, especially since the woman didn't pay any attention to him. That just made his feelings stronger. He constantly thought about her. Sometimes he was very happy. More often he was sad. When he saw her with another man, he became extremely jealous. He began to go to church, trying to console himself with religion.

One evening he went to an elaborate fancy dress ball. The dancers swirled about the room, but the man didn't feel like joining them. He only wanted to be with his love—but he was too bashful to ask her to dance. Occasionally, he would catch a glimpse of her, smiling happily at her different partners. Finally, he gave up and went home.

He took a walk in the countryside, hoping that peaceful images of nature would help soothe his pain. Off in the distance, he heard two shepherds piping to each other. But he didn't find the calm that he hoped for. He kept remembering his beloved. A storm rolled in, reflecting his inner turmoil. After it passed, the sun began

to set. One of the shepherds began piping again. The answer this time wasn't the other shepherd, but more thunder. The storm was returning.

One day the young man heard that his beloved was having an affair with someone else. He snapped. He couldn't take it any longer. He murdered the young woman. He was captured and sentenced to death. On the day of his execution, he was escorted from his cell and put into a horse-drawn cart. A band marched along behind him. People lining the streets hooted and jeered at him. He arrived at the scaffold. With his hands tied behind his back, he slowly mounted the few steps. Then he knelt under the guillotine, the sharp blade hanging over his head. He had one last thought of his beloved. Then the heavy blade dropped. His severed head bounced a few times on the wooden planks and rolled into a basket.

But that wasn't the end. A bizarre assembly of witches, ghosts, goblins, and other awful monsters gathered for his funeral. It was like a huge Halloween party as they all danced around the graves in the cemetery. After a while his beloved appeared, but she was no longer young and beautiful. She was old, ugly, and deformed. All the horrible creatures howled their greetings to her, then they had one final dance as bells tolled solemnly for the dead man.

If all this sounds like a fantastic, unbelievable story, most of it is. It is the program, or plot, of *Symphonie fantastique,* which literally means "fantastic symphony." It was composed by Hector Berlioz (pronounced BEAR-lee-oze).

Symphonie fantastique was inspired by real-life events. When Berlioz was a young man and living in Paris, he often went to performances of operas and plays. In 1827 he watched Shakespeare's play *Hamlet.* One of the main characters in the play is Ophelia, a young woman who falls in love with Prince Hamlet. Hamlet rejects

William Shakespeare (1564–1616), an English playwright and poet, wrote such famous works as Hamlet, Romeo and Juliet, Othello, and Macbeth.

her. She goes mad and kills herself. In the performance Berlioz saw, the role of Ophelia was played by an Irish actress named Harriet Smithson.

Like the man in *Symphonie fantastique,* Berlioz experienced love at first sight. His feelings became even stronger a few days later when he saw Harriet perform the role of Juliet in *Romeo and Juliet.* But his love seemed doomed. Harriet was famous all over the city of Paris, while hardly anyone had heard of the young composer. It didn't matter to him. He became obsessed and started writing passionate love letters to her.

She ignored them.

He tried to impress Harriet by presenting a concert of his own music. It was a daring move, because no one in France had ever tried doing that before. He hoped that such a presentation would convince her that he was a dramatic artist who was worthy of her notice.

It didn't work. She still ignored him. She didn't even know what he looked like. In fact, she was probably a little frightened. One night he tried to go backstage and meet her after she had performed in a play. She refused to see him and ordered the guard to throw him out.

After so many rejections, most people would give up. Not Berlioz. He somehow decided that she was testing him, that she was deliberately avoiding him to see how serious he was. He kept writing to her.

Scenarios like this, with unknown people trying to impress famous actors, happen even today. For example, a young man named John Hinckley saw Jodie Foster in the movie *Taxi Driver.* He wanted to do something that would make her take notice of him— so he tried to assassinate U.S. President Ronald Reagan in 1981. After Hinckley was sent to prison, he mailed a series of bizarre letters to Foster. People who have this kind of obsession are often dangerous. In 1989, a young actress named Rebecca Schaeffer was murdered by a stalker.

Fortunately, Hector Berlioz didn't present a physical danger to Harriet. When she went back to London without ever having met him, he was heartbroken. He wanted revenge. But he took out his grief and anger in music rather than through violence. That was when he began writing *Symphonie fantastique.*

This tendency to put his emotions directly into music marks Berlioz as among the first of what are called Romantic composers. For the Romantics, expressing their emotions was the most important aspect of their art.

Eventually Berlioz and Harriet would meet. But the outcome wouldn't be anything like what Berlioz had imagined it would be.

A FAMOUS FRENCH WRITER

Alexandre Dumas

Born in 1802, French writer Alexandre Dumas (DOO-mah) was an almost exact contemporary of Hector Berlioz. His stories, such as *The Three Musketeers, The Count of Monte Cristo,* and *The Man in the Iron Mask,* are not only fun to read but also fun to watch—they have been made into more than 200 movies. Dumas's grandfather was a French nobleman who lived in the Caribbean country of Haiti, where he married a black slave. Dumas's father became a general in Napoléon Bonaparte's army but died when Alexandre was four. Though the boy grew up in poverty, he found a job with the future French king Louis-Philippe when he moved to Paris.

He soon turned to writing. His first success came in 1829 with the play *Henri III et sa cour (Henry III and His Court).* The advent of daily newspapers in the 1830s brought about his greatest recognition. Publishers began to include stories that were written in serial form. These stories were a mixture of historical facts and made-up episodes. Each chapter ended with a suspenseful scene, which left people wanting to buy the next edition to see what came next. Dumas was successful in writing these serials, but he earned even more money by compiling the stories into book form. Even though people had already read the stories in the newspapers, they enjoyed the adventures so much that they eagerly bought the books.

Dumas lived as adventurously as his heroes. He traveled a great deal, fought in wars and in duels, had romances with many women, and even built a huge mansion outside Paris—which he named Château de Monte Cristo. He wrote more than 250 books and plays, employing a staff of several dozen researchers to help him. He made a great deal of money and spent it almost as rapidly.

He died of a stroke on December 5, 1870. Today the Château de Monte Cristo is a popular tourist site.

This portrait of Hector Berlioz was probably created about the time that he composed Symphonie fantastique. The grotesque images behind him are some of the horrible creatures who dance at the hero's funeral in the final movement of the work.

CHAPTER

2

First Love

Louis-Hector Berlioz was born on December 11, 1803, in the small hill town of La Côte-Saint-André, between Lyon and Grenoble in southeastern France. His parents were Marie-Antoinette-Joséphine and Louis-Joseph Berlioz. Hector was the first of the couple's six children, but only he and two of his sisters would survive to adulthood.

His father was the town doctor, and his medical practice yielded a good income. He had also inherited some property. Hector grew up in a comfortable, financially secure household.

Biographer D. Kern Holoman describes the Berlioz home, which is still standing, as "a rambling town house on the main street, of two stories with an attic and any number of nooks and crannies, enveloping three sides of a courtyard. It is fashioned of masonry and stone. An entry hall leads up into the living area and down into a cellar, where the young composer held his chamber music sessions. The main dwelling rooms were on the first floor above the entry level; bedrooms and Dr. Berlioz' consulting rooms were in other parts of the house."[1]

The "nooks and crannies" must have been fun, out-of-the-way places for young Hector to play in during his first few years.

At some point, perhaps when Hector was as young as six, the family sent him to the local school for his education. While no one knows how long he stayed, it probably wasn't for more than a year or two. It soon became obvious to Louis-Joseph that his son was too bright to benefit from the curriculum there. It was equally obvious who the best teacher would be: Louis-Joseph himself. He was an intelligent man with many interests besides medicine. Because he maintained a home office, he was close at hand and could easily spend time with his son between visits from his patients. As we would say today, Hector Berlioz was homeschooled. Under his father's direction, he studied a wide variety of subjects, including mathematics, astronomy, geography, and literature.

His mother provided him with a different kind of education. She was a devout Catholic and took her children to daily mass and to communion on Sundays.

Hector and his father read many of the same books together. Some were classic Greek and Latin works. Others emphasized travel. Biographies of important composers were added to the list as the youngster became more and more interested in music. At first, his father encouraged this interest. He purchased a flute for Hector and provided some basic instruction.

When Hector was 12, the family took a summer vacation at his grandfather's home in a nearby village. The memory would remain with him for the rest of his life, because there he spied an 18-year-old girl named Estelle Duboeuf.

As Holoman writes, "Berlioz was smitten with the handsome girl: her hair, her good looks, and above all her pink boots. She was standing, he recalled, on a rock, her hand resting on the trunk of a cherry tree."[2]

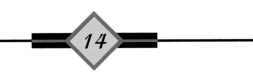

Even much later in his life, Berlioz could remember every detail of the scene and how he felt. "I was conscious of an electric shock. I loved her."[3]

It was love at first sight, a pattern that would recur during his life. But he didn't say anything to Estelle, and she had no idea of the depth of his feelings.

Two years later he began formal music instruction, taking lessons from a violinist named Imbert. Imbert offered voice and flute lessons to the town's middle-class boys. During this time Berlioz began writing some of his own music. But this early creative period was not to last. Imbert's son committed suicide, and the grieving father left town.

In the spring of 1819, Berlioz began taking lessons from a Monsieur François-Xavier Dorant. Dorant was an excellent guitar player, and Berlioz mastered this instrument as well. He wrote several songs soon afterward, and they were published. Berlioz remained grateful to Dorant for his entire life. He referred to him much later as "my old guitar teacher whom I haven't seen for twenty years."[4]

His father wasn't excited. It was one thing to play an instrument for recreation, but Hector's increasing interest in music suggested that he was thinking of making a career of it. At that time, polite society in rural France frowned on such an occupation. It was something appropriate for girls, not bright young men.

And there was another, more practical reason. One of Hector's younger brothers had just died. The death put some pressure on Hector as a male to continue the family line, and that would involve one important thing: a steady, reliable job. Composing didn't qualify. Medicine did. His parents wanted him to go to Paris and begin attending medical school, following in his father's footsteps. However, Hector had almost no interest in medicine. He must have felt like he was in a pickle.

His father decided not to play hardball. To make the medical route more attractive, he did what many parents have done in similar situations: He made a deal with his son. He told Hector that if he began studying an anatomy book at home, he could have a new flute. The studying wasn't easy. Hector was a sensitive boy with a lively imagination.

"This new knowledge came hard," says author Jacques Barzun. "It gave Hector creepy feelings to recollect or imagine the last struggles of the dying."[5]

Somehow Hector managed to overcome these feelings. He made an agreement with his parents. He would go to Paris and study medicine. They would provide him with a generous allowance.

It was an agreement that wouldn't last very long.

Berlioz's family home in the French provincial town of La Côte-Saint-André as it appeared in the 19th century (left) and in a recent photograph (right). It was roomy and comfortable, with plenty of space for young Hector to hold small musical concerts, for his father to conduct his medical practice, and for the family to relax. A memorial plaque donated by townspeople soon after the composer's death identifies the home for visitors.

WHO INVENTED BASEBALL?

"Caught in a pickle" and "playing hardball" are just two of many baseball terms that are used in everyday speech. "He really threw me a curve" or "it came out of left field" mean something unexpected happened. If you "go to bat" for someone, you support that person. You "cover all the bases" when you are well prepared. And you "hit a grand slam" when you do something spectacularly successful.

Doubleday Field, June 12, 1939

While Berlioz never played baseball or even saw a game, it was invented during his lifetime. Many people believe that the first game of baseball was played in the small town of Cooperstown, New York, in 1839 under the direction of Abner Doubleday. According to the story, Doubleday changed a game called "town ball" by scratching out the shape of a diamond, adding bases (which gave the new game its name), and using a pitcher and catcher. In later life, Doubleday became a distinguished military officer with the U.S. Army. He is credited with firing the first cannon at Fort Sumter, South Carolina, at the start of the Civil War.

Others emphasize the importance of a New York banker named Alexander Cartwright. In 1845, Cartwright organized the Knickerbocker Baseball Club and chaired the committee that introduced three important changes to the game. One was establishing the distance of 90 feet between bases. The second was dividing the playing field into fair and foul areas. The third was changing the way a base runner was put out: Instead of hitting him with a thrown ball, he would be tagged with the ball.

Within a few years, Cartwright's version of baseball had spread to many other parts of the country. Cartwright himself helped popularize the game. In 1849, he journeyed west as part of the California gold rush. Along the way, he taught people how to play. After reaching California, he crossed the Pacific Ocean to Honolulu, Hawaii. He introduced the game there and eventually became one of the city's most important inhabitants.

Alexander Cartwright's baseball

Baseball honors both men. The Baseball Hall of Fame is located in Cooperstown. Cartwright was inducted in 1938, three years after it was founded.

This 19th century painting depicts Claude-Joseph Rouget de Lisle in a performance of "La Marseillaise," the stirring patriotic song that he composed. Berlioz wrote an arrangement of the composition. "La Marseillaise" became the French national anthem in 1879.

CHAPTER

3

Musician or Physician

To travel in France in the 1820s, it was necessary to obtain what was known as an internal passport. Because photography was in its infancy, the passport contained a written description of the holder. Berlioz was five feet, four inches tall. That is short by today's standards, but probably about average nearly 200 years ago. According to his passport, he had "an ordinary forehead; grey eyes; well-formed nose; medium mouth; beginnings of a beard; round chin; oval face; ruddy complexion; no distinguishing marks."[1]

It wouldn't take him long to begin distinguishing himself in his career, anyway. Or to lose interest in medicine.

He took an apartment with his cousin Alphonse Robert and enrolled in an anatomy class. One of the requirements was to dissect a corpse.

Robert purchased a corpse, and the two young men set off to the morgue for their introduction to the mysteries of the human body. It turned out to be a quick visit for Hector. He wrote, "At the sight of that terrible charnel-house—the fragments of limbs, the grinning faces and gaping skulls, the bloody quagmire underfoot and the atrocious smell it gave off, the swarms of sparrows wrangling over scraps of lung, the rats in their corner gnawing the bleeding vertebrae—such a feeling of revulsion possessed me that I leapt through the window of the dissecting-room and fled for home as though Death and all his hideous train were at my heels."[2]

The horrific scene greatly affected him. "I firmly resolved to die rather than enter the career that had been forced on me," he said.[3] But somehow he made himself return to the morgue. This is how he described the way he dealt with the situation:

"I had become as callous to the revolting scene as a veteran soldier. I even found some pleasure in rummaging in the gaping breast of an unfortunate corpse for the lungs, with which to feed the winged inhabitants of that charming place."

" 'Well done!' cried Robert, laughing. 'You are growing quite humane! Feeding the little birds!' "

" 'And my bounty extends to all nature,' I answered, 'throwing a shoulder blade to a great rat that was staring at me with famished eyes.' "[4]

Ripping bodies apart to feed ravenous animals and birds wasn't the best way to become a doctor. By then, it was even more apparent to the young man that he wasn't cut out for the practice of medicine. He began attending the opera regularly, and it made a profoundly positive impression on him. He soon discovered that the music library of the Paris Conservatory—the leading academy of music in the country—was open to anyone who wanted to use it. Berlioz began spending hours on end there. One of his main activities was copying out the scores of operas by Christoph Gluck, who had an especial influence on him. It was evident to Berlioz that composing was what he really wanted to do. Soon afterward, he began studying with an older composer named Jean-François Le Sueur.

Christoph Gluck (1714-1787) was a German composer who lived and worked in nearly every major music center in Europe. His primary fame was the result of the numerous operas that he wrote.

Berlioz went home the following spring. It was an awkward homecoming. His father's objections were practical. Composing would provide an unstable income. His mother's were of a different sort. She said that what he was doing was sinful, that he was "setting his feet on the broad road that leads to disgrace in this world and damnation in the next."[5] Medicine, of course, was more honorable and steady.

Berlioz found himself in a dilemma. He needed his parents' support, both financially and emotionally. Yet he hated medicine. In addition, Le Sueur had expressed confidence in him. Somehow Berlioz managed to find the inner strength to believe in himself and in what he wanted to do.

Somehow he managed to spend enough time on medicine to obtain his bachelor's degree in 1824. Soon afterward he tried to have one of his compositions performed. The rehearsal was a disaster and the scheduled performance was canceled. For his father, it was clear proof that his son had no future as a composer. He cut off Hector's allowance.

The young man wasn't deterred. Early the following year his composition was performed successfully. Both the Paris public and his teacher Le Sueur were impressed. His parents weren't.

In 1826 he was admitted to the conservatory as a student. He also applied for the Prix de Rome. The winner of this contest in

musical composition would spend three years in Rome studying music. Berlioz didn't get past the preliminary round. He wasn't having much luck anywhere else either. He was trying to write operas, but no one was interested.

Somehow he managed to scrape together enough money to make ends meet. He borrowed from his friends, gave lessons, and wrote an occasional newspaper article. At one point he even sang in a musical theater, though it was such a humiliating experience that he kept it secret from everyone.

Then he saw Harriet Smithson for the first time.

While he was struggling with his passion for Harriet, he was still studying music. In 1828 he discovered the works of Ludwig van Beethoven, who would have a tremendous influence on Berlioz's musical development.

"Beethoven opened before me a new world of music," he wrote.[6] It was the first time that he had gone beyond vocal music to the emotional power that instrumental music could convey. It was perfect timing.

"He saw at once, amid the emotional impact of Beethoven's music, that he could promote himself and direct concerts of symphonic music whereas the doors of all opera houses were firmly closed to him," writes author Hugh Macdonald.[7]

Harriet kept reappearing in Paris theaters, but she was as distant and unavailable as ever. Finally everything exploded inside the young composer. He began writing *Symphonie fantastique*. Because he adapted some music that he had already written, it took him just a few months, and he finished it early in 1830. There was one genuine innovation in the piece. He represented the "beloved" (Harriet) by a short musical phrase called the idée fixe (fixed idea), which appears in every movement and helps unify the entire

symphony. He showed his despair in the final movement (which he called "Dream of a Witches' Sabbath") by turning the idée fixe into an ugly, grotesque parody of itself.

Writing *Symphonie fantastique* may have helped him quell his feelings for Harriet. There was something else, too.

"Horrible truths, revealed beyond the possibility of doubt, have set me on the way to recovery, and I think it will be as complete as my obstinate nature will permit," he wrote.[8]

At least some of these "horrible truths" may have come from an 18-year-old pianist named Camille Moke. She had been romantically involved with one of Berlioz's friends, Ferdinand Hiller, but suddenly took up with Berlioz. She apparently helped her own cause by telling the trusting young man a series of lies about Harriet. All of his frustrated energy then became focused on Camille. Harriet wasn't available. Camille was.

"All that love offers that is most tender and delicate, I have from Camille," he wrote. "My enchanting sylph, my Ariel, my life, seems to love me more than ever: as for me, her mother keeps on saying that if she had read in a novel the description of love like mine she would not believe it true."[9]

The summer of 1830 was especially momentous, both for Berlioz personally and for France in general. A brief popular revolution in July brought King Louis-Philippe to power. He was considered to be in favor of democratic reforms. In the midst of all the confusion, Berlioz was trying to finish his composition for what he had vowed would be his fifth and final attempt to win the Prix de Rome.

Berlioz was also caught up in the spirit of revolution. He quickly completed an arrangement of "La Marseillaise." The song had been written in 1792 by a French army officer named Claude-Joseph

Rouget de Lisle, who wanted to inspire the soldiers after France declared war on Austria and Prussia. Though it was composed in Strasbourg, it got its name when volunteers from the city of Marseilles sang it constantly on their way to join the main army in Paris. It was adopted as a national song in 1795, but because of its spirit of revolution, it was soon banned. Berlioz's lively arrangement and the spirit of the times brought it new popularity. In 1879 the song became the French national anthem.

Claude-Joseph Rouget de Lisle (1760-1836) is famous as the composer of "La Marseillaise," the French national anthem.

This print depicts Rouget de Lisle singing "La Marseillaise" before the mayor of Strasbourg, who had asked him to write a marching song after the French declared war on Austria and Prussia in 1792. It was an immediate hit and spread throughout France.

In August, Berlioz was finally awarded the Prix de Rome. *Symphonie fantastique* made its debut in December and was well received. Both of these successes impressed Camille's mother, who allowed her daughter to become engaged to the young composer. They exchanged rings and set a wedding date 18 months away. Hector's life finally seemed to be going the way he wanted it to. He was 27, in love, and appeared to be on the verge of a successful career as a composer.

But as so often happens, it didn't take long for his life to change direction.

THE U.S. NATIONAL ANTHEM

Francis Scott Key

Like "La Marseillaise," the U.S. national anthem came about because of a battle. On August 24, 1814, British troops burned the White House and other important buildings in Washington, D.C., the nation's capital. President James Madison narrowly escaped being captured.

An elderly Maryland physician named William Beanes was not so fortunate. He was captured a few days later and taken aboard a British ship. His friends were afraid that he would be hanged, so they asked a respected young lawyer named Francis Scott Key and Colonel John Skinner to go to the British ship and plead for Beanes's release.

Key and Skinner were successful. The British agreed to let Beanes go, but not right away. They were about to attack nearby Baltimore. The three Americans knew too much about their plans. They would have to stay with the British until the attack was over.

Early on the morning of September 13, the British began bombarding Fort McHenry, at the entrance of Baltimore Harbor. Waving over the fort's walls was a huge American flag. Measuring 42 feet by 30 feet, it had been sewn by Mary Young Pickersgill and her 13-year-old daughter, Caroline. Each of the 15 stars measured two feet across.

The bombardment lasted all day and into the night. Some of the British cannons fired 200-pound bombs, many of which exploded in midair. The British also fired rockets that left red trails behind them as they headed toward the fort.

Key, Beanes, and Skinner waited anxiously through the night. At dawn, they looked toward Fort McHenry. The huge flag was still flying. The British attack had failed.

The three men were released. As he sailed back home, Key pulled out a used envelope. An amateur poet, he jotted down a poem that described his feelings about what he had seen. Called "Defence of Fort McHenry," it was published in several papers. People liked it so much that they gave it a tune. Ironically, the tune was a popular English drinking song called "To Anacreon in Heaven." Not long afterward, the name of the song was changed to "The Star-Spangled Banner."

On March 3, 1931, "The Star-Spangled Banner" was officially adopted as the U.S. national anthem.

This portrait of Hector Berlioz dates from the latter part of his life. His melancholy expression reflects a number of disappointments and personal losses that plagued him during this period.

CHAPTER

4

The Grand Passion Returns

O n his way to Rome, Berlioz spent a few weeks visiting his family. Now that he was successful, his family was much warmer toward him. But all was not completely well. Hiller, who had remained close to Berlioz despite losing Camille to him, sent his friend an ominous letter. He wrote that Camille's behavior wasn't entirely what would one would expect from a young woman who was engaged to be married. Berlioz was upset, but he still departed as scheduled for Rome. He looked forward to receiving several letters from Camille when he arrived there. But there weren't any.

He spent several weeks trying to do some work and anxiously visiting the post office. There still weren't any letters from Camille. When he could no longer take the strain, he decided to return to Paris. He got as far as Florence before becoming ill. After a week in bed, he recovered enough to wander through the city.

Finally he received a letter, but it wasn't from Camille. It was from her mother.

She informed him that Camille had married another man. In an oddity, he had the same first name. He was 53-year-old Camille Pleyel, who was also a composer. More importantly, he owned a

very successful piano manufacturing company and lived in a big house. As a husband, therefore, Pleyel, even though he was 34 years older than his bride, was a much better prospect than the still relatively unknown Berlioz.

Berlioz went ballistic.

"Two tears of rage started from my eyes," he wrote. "In that instant I knew my course: It was to go at once to Paris and there kill without compunction two guilty women and one guilty man."[1]

His plan was to disguise himself as a maid to get close enough to the newlyweds and Camille's mother. He would shoot them with two pistols, which he swiftly obtained. Then he would commit suicide.

What saved four persons from death was the speed of travel at that time. Berlioz immediately boarded a horse-drawn carriage, but he traveled fewer than a hundred miles per day. He was still angry when he reached the Italian seaport city of Genoa and reportedly tried to commit suicide by throwing himself into the ocean. But a few days later, just before he reached the French coastal city of Nice, his anger subsided.

He spent a great deal of time at the beach; met a young woman, with whom he had a brief affair; and described the ensuing three weeks as the happiest of his life. He wandered along the beach with a sketchbook, until he attracted the notice of the local police. They considered what he was doing as highly suspicious behavior. They gave him two choices: go back where he came from or go to jail.

Berlioz returned to Rome, where he met another young composer, Felix Mendelssohn. Though they had a common interest in music, the young German wasn't impressed with Berlioz. Mendelssohn thought Berlioz talked too much about women.

In all, Berlioz spent more than a year in Rome, much of it wandering through the countryside. Those wanderings gave him the inspiration for several works, both then and in the future.

In May 1832, he left Rome. He spent nearly six months in La Côte-Saint-André visiting his family before returning to Paris. When he arrived, he discovered that his previous rooms were no longer available. He went across the street and found a very odd thing. There was a vacant apartment there. The previous occupant had moved out just a few days before. Her name was Harriet Smithson.

German composer Felix Mendelssohn (1809-1847) remains one of the most popular figures in classical music. He is best-known for his "Wedding March," which is played at the end of many weddings in the United States and Europe.

Since her triumph in 1827, Harriet had fallen on hard times. After returning to England, her acting troupe had gone bankrupt. Now she was back in Paris, but the old magic had disappeared. The French public wasn't interested in hearing Shakespeare's plays in English anymore. Harriet was struggling to make ends meet.

None of that mattered to Berlioz. It seemed like fate. Memories of his former love came surging back with the force of a tidal wave. He decided to show his feelings in a grand manner. In early December, he put on a concert that included *Symphonie fantastique*. He arranged for a special seat for Harriet. Surely she would realize that she had been the inspiration for the symphony.

This time, putting on a concert for her benefit worked. Harriet was impressed enough to agree to be introduced to Berlioz a few days later. This time Harriet was very available. Their affair moved quickly after that. Berlioz wrote ecstatic letters to his friends, telling of his love for Harriet and assuring them that she was feeling the same way toward him.

As Shakespeare wrote in his play *A Midsummer Night's Dream,* "the course of true love never did run smooth." Despite Berlioz's happy letters, the courtship was anything but calm. When Berlioz proposed marriage, both families were vehemently opposed. Under French law, Berlioz then had to go to court to get permission. There were other obstacles. Berlioz didn't know much English and Harriet could barely speak French. She had huge debts. She broke her leg getting out of a carriage and couldn't work. As the weeks and months dragged on, Harriet began to have second thoughts. Berlioz was not above using a little emotional blackmail. Once he threatened to take poison in front of her. Another time he told her that he was going to travel to Germany with a young woman as his companion.

Harriet relented. She and Berlioz were married on October 3, 1833. After six years of emotional anguish, it appeared that Hector Berlioz would finally be happy.

WALKING A
TIGHTROPE

Berlioz may have felt as if he had been walking on a tightrope ever since he met Harriet. A quarter of a century later, one of his countrymen would walk a real tightrope and become an instant celebrity.

In 1859, a circus performer named Claude Blondin was touring the United States. He ran newspaper ads announcing that he would cross Niagara Falls on a tightrope. Thousands of people traveled to the falls on the morning of June 30 to watch him. Many believed that he would fall into the rushing water far below and be swept to his death.

Blondin had been born in 1824. At an early age he saw a circus tightrope walker. Like modern kids, he wanted to try what he had just seen. His father put up a rope in their yard and the youngster began practicing. He also went to a gymnastics school. Soon he began tightrope walking in public. Because he was just five, he was called the Little Wonder.

His father died four years later, so Charles had to keep performing to support himself. By the time he was ready to cross Niagara Falls, he had been tightrope walking for 30 years.

Even though the rope stretched for 1,100 feet—about a fifth of a mile—he felt confident. Holding a pole more than 30 feet long to help balance himself, he made the crossing in about five minutes. That was too easy. On that day and on several other occasions, he added variations. He crossed backward. Blindfolded. At night. On stilts. Carrying a passenger. One time he even packed a portable stove. Halfway across, he stopped, cooked an omelet, and then ate it.

These stunts made him famous. He was asked to perform in many other places, and he reportedly made a half million dollars annually.

He was never seriously injured during his career. He eventually retired and died in his own bed in 1897.

This is a portrait of Harriet Smithson at the age of 19 or 20, when she was beginning her acting career. For several years she was extremely popular in France, but by the time of her marriage to Berlioz she was struggling to find work.

CHAPTER 5

Reality Strikes

There is an old saying that goes, "Be careful what you wish for. You may get it."

Berlioz got what he wanted. He was married to Harriet Smithson. But reality turned out to be very different from fantasy. It was one thing to be in love with someone who appeared on stage. It was entirely different to live with that person 24 hours a day.

At first, their life together seemed to run smoothly. Hector's family grew to accept the marriage. Harriet gave birth to a son, Louis, on August 14, 1834. In early 1836, Berlioz wrote to his sister, "Here is my life in four words: I am very happy—to have the best and most-loved wife in the world."[1]

Over the next few years, he composed several of his best-known works. But this apparent success masked some underlying uneasiness.

His letter to his sister had continued, "But I suffer greatly from all the privations I see her enduring without complaint; by her isolation, and above all, by the loss of her immense talent. Her forced inaction is killing her."[2]

Harriet had put on a great deal of weight and was no longer able to perform in public. Because neither could speak the other's language well, it was hard to communicate. Berlioz wasn't making much money, and taking on Harriet's debts created financial hardships.

One solution was to take an additional job as a music critic. Though Berlioz is now regarded as one of the best writers about music of all time, it didn't come easy. Describing his writing process, he revealed he was "like a schoolboy who cannot do his homework." While the following may sound overly dramatic, it could easily apply to anyone who has had to write a class report: "About the fourth line or so I get up, walk around the room, look out into the streets, take up a book. . . . My brain seemed ready to burst. My veins were burning. Sometimes I remained with my elbows on the table, holding my head in both my hands. Sometimes I strode up and down like a soldier on guard in a frost 25 degrees below zero. . . . And when, on turning around, my eyes fell on that accursed title inscribed at the head of that accursed sheet of paper, still blank and obstinately waiting for the words with which it was supposed to be covered, I felt simply overcome by despair."[3]

But just like modern schoolboys and professional writers, he always managed to get it done. In fact, for several years he was better known to Paris music lovers as a critic than as a composer.

This, of course, did not satisfy him. Berlioz had long felt that the best way to become recognized was to write an opera. He completed *Benvenuto Cellini,* which was influenced to a large extent by his travels in Italy. It premiered in 1838 but was performed only three times and was considered a failure.

A large loan from famous violinist Niccolò Paganini helped to keep the family financially solvent. Early in 1839, Berlioz was hired as librarian at the Paris Conservatory. In that position, he was also

able to compose. The result was a large work for orchestra and chorus based on Shakespeare's *Romeo and Juliet,* which had so ignited his imagination when Harriet had performed the role of Juliet in 1827.

But Berlioz's relations with his real-life Juliet were steadily disintegrating. He and Harriet were drifting further and further apart.

As writer Peter Bloom notes, "After the first years of their marriage, Harriet began to take care neither of the house nor of herself; she had difficulty raising her son and supervising her servants; frequently ill, she kept the composer from sleeping and berated him in lengthy nocturnal tirades exacerbated by large doses of alcohol. . . . It was not long before what had been a heavenly goal [gaining the love of Harriet] became a burden very much of this earth."[4]

Niccolò Paganini (1782-1840) was considered the greatest violinist of his era. He toured extensively for many years, dazzling audiences with his technique and the force of his personality. He also composed numerous works for the violin.

And this burden was dragging Hector Berlioz further and further down.

By 1841, Berlioz's life appeared to be in shambles. Almost none of his works were being performed. The only steady job he had was as conservatory librarian. His marriage with Harriet had become hopeless.

He began to hear reports that his music was being played often in foreign countries, an indication that he was more popular there than in Paris. So he began touring. By then he had met a singer named Marie Recio, and she became his constant companion.

On top of everything else, the knowledge that her husband was unfaithful was devastating for Harriet. Her health continued to worsen. Berlioz didn't completely abandon her, however. He sent enough money to support her and their son.

Unlike Harriet and Camille, Marie didn't inspire any great music. Berlioz never felt the same passion for her that he had for the other two women. In fact, he would be with her nearly 10 years before he would write anything else memorable. During this time his professional life was insecure. He traveled to different countries such as Germany, England, Belgium, Austria, and Czechoslovakia. He was treated almost everywhere with a great deal of enthusiasm both as an original composer and an excellent conductor, then come home to indifference in Paris.

"In Paris music too often speaks to morons, barbarians and the deaf," he wrote.[5]

In 1849 he helped found the Société Philharmonique, a Parisian imitation of the London Philharmonic Society, which he had visited two years earlier. But it didn't do well and failed in just over a year.

He went back to London for the second time in 1851 and achieved a certain measure of fame, conducting several concerts the following year. There was one very sour note. Camille, the pianist to whom he had once been engaged, was a soloist in one of the performances. Even though she had turned out to be an unfaithful wife and her husband had left her within four years of their marriage, Berlioz was still bitter. He complained about the quality of her playing. She said that he was a terrible conductor.

Berlioz soon had much more to worry about than the quality of his conducting. ◆

CINCO DE MAYO

Mexico declared its independence from Spain in 1810 and drove out the final remaining Spanish soldiers in 1821. But the country was unable to establish a stable government. In addition, the 1846-1848 war with the United States cost Mexico about half its territory. Meanwhile, Mexico ran up sizable debts with other nations.

Taking advantage of the U.S. Civil War, Spain, England, and France sent troops to Mexico to enforce payment of those debts. Spain and England soon withdrew, but the French remained.

On May 5, 1862, an outnumbered, disorganized band of Mexican troops faced a French army near the town of Puebla. Against all expectations, the Mexicans won the battle.

The win had little effect on the war, as the French emperor Napoléon III sent many more troops. Mexico City was soon captured. Some Mexicans, who distrusted the reforms of the liberal Benito Juárez, invited an Austrian nobleman named Ferdinand Maximilian to come and rule the country. When Maximilian and his wife, Carlota, landed in June 1864, they were shocked to find that Mexico was in the midst of a civil war. The only thing that kept them in power was the French army.

However, in 1866 the U.S. government demanded that the French withdraw their troops. With the U.S. threat from the borders and the internal opposition from Juárez, Napoléon began withdrawing his army. They boarded French warships that came to pick them up. One of the ships was commanded by Berlioz's son Louis.

Maximilian could have gone home as well, but he chose to remain. In May 1867, he and the few Mexican troops who remained loyal to him were defeated. He was captured and executed a month later. It would be the last time that Mexico had a foreign ruler.

Over the years, many Mexicans remembered the date of the battle of Puebla and the heroism of their troops. The victory there became a source of national pride. Today, Cinco de Mayo, the Fifth of May, is widely celebrated, especially in U.S. cities that have a large Hispanic population.

Five famous artistic figures in France are immortalized in wax. From left, they are novelist George Sand, Berlioz, Harriet Smithson, pianist and composer Franz Liszt, and painter Eugene Delacroix.

Final Troubles

When Berlioz was traveling, Harriet became so weak that she couldn't even speak. She died on March 3, 1854. Berlioz was at her bedside when the end came.

"Berlioz's grief was genuine and mixed with pity for Harriet's misfortunes—her broken heart, her vanished beauty, her ruined health and loss of speech and movement," writes Robert Clarson-Leach.[1]

Just over seven months later, on October 19, Berlioz married Marie Recio. The previous day he completed his *Mémoires*. Interestingly, Marie is hardly ever mentioned in the book.

Much of Berlioz's energy over the next few years went into an opera called *Les Troyens* (The Trojans). He finished it in 1858, but it would be five years before it was performed.

By this time, Berlioz was starting to show symptoms of physical decline. He suffered from a disease he called intestinal neuralgia. While the malady isn't recognized medically today, the pain was real enough. On the other hand, he became closer to his son, and in 1862, he composed a comic opera called *Béatrice and Bénédict*. It would be his final composition.

Marie died of a heart attack a few months later. It was a severe shock to Berlioz. Her death was totally unexpected. It was also the first time that he had been alone in nearly 20 years.

In 1863 he suffered another shock. *Les Troyens* was presented, and it was a success. However, the production consisted of less than half of what he had written, despite what the producers had promised him. He was deeply disappointed.

Heartbreaks kept mounting. A friend purchased a burial vault for him, so he had to dig up and rebury the coffins of both of his wives. That wasn't difficult with Marie, but Harriet's remains were a different story. The coffin was rotting and a gravedigger yanked up the boards. Then, with Berlioz watching in horror, "The gravedigger bent down and with his two hands picked up the head, already separated from the body—the ungarlanded, hairless and withered head of 'poor Ophelia'—and placed it in a new coffin ready for it at the edge of the pit. Then, bending down again, he lifted with great difficulty and gathered into his arms the headless trunk and limbs, a blackish mass which the shroud still clung to, and which resembled a lump of pitch wrapped in a damp sack. There was a dull sound and a terrible smell."[2]

It is probably no wonder that Berlioz wrote, "I am in my sixty-first year; past hopes, past illusion, past high thoughts and lofty conceptions. My son is almost always far away from me. I am alone. My contempt for the folly and baseness of mankind, my hatred of its atrocious cruelty, have never been so intense. And I say hourly to Death: 'When you will.' What is he waiting for?"[3]

There was one final ray of hope. In his despair, he remembered his youthful passions and discovered where Estelle Duboeuf was living. He went to visit her in 1864. She had long since married and had several children, and she had been widowed.

Even though it had been nearly five decades since she had made that first impression on him, Berlioz's feelings were still fresh.

"My soul leapt out towards its idol the moment I saw her, as if she had still been in the splendor of her beauty," he wrote.[4]

Though Estelle was astonished to learn of his adolescent passion for her, she became an understanding and supportive friend. They exchanged letters regularly for the rest of his life.

In 1866, he had a visit from his son. Louis was now a ship captain in the French navy. When they parted, both men realized that Hector's ill health could make this their final meeting. It was, but the cause wasn't Hector.

Louis's ship was part of the French fleet that originally sailed to Mexico to support the shaky rule of the emperor Maximilian. The fleet then evacuated French troops as Napoléon III withdrew his army. When Louis's ship docked in Havana in 1867, he contracted yellow fever and died. He was only 33.

Berlioz collapsed when he heard the news. He burned many of his personal papers and sank deeper into depression. He traveled to Russia to enjoy a final fleeting moment of fame, but his health steadily worsened. He died on March 8, 1869. He was laid to rest next to Harriet and Marie.

At his funeral, one speaker said, "Berlioz will remain one of the great symbols of our century. . . . [In his belief in] a consummate ideal founded upon truth, he was one of the most vigorous representatives of the new spirit of the age."[5]

Today, we might call Berlioz an idealist.

"He strove for an ideal world in which the greatest music was permanently accessible to a discriminating public, and from which

'cretins and toads' and the riff-raff of popular music were excluded," writes Hugh Macdonald.[6]

But the ideal didn't materialize. MacDonald continues that Berlioz in his final years "had come to realize that the modern world, the world in which he had to fight for a living as a composer, was not approaching his ideals but receding from them at an accelerating pace."[7]

Still, Berlioz always remained true to those ideals.

"Should one offer me a hundred thousand francs to sign my name to one of those works that are today immensely successful, I would angrily refuse," he wrote. "That is how I am made."[8]

EUGENE DELACROIX

Berlioz had yet another reason for sadness during the seemingly endless string of losses he suffered during his final decade. His friend, the painter Eugene Delacroix, died on August 13, 1863.

Both men are considered as leaders of the Romantic Movement in art. Delacroix painted many leading artists of the day, including pianist/composer Frédéric Chopin, novelist George Sand, violinist Niccolò Paganini and Berlioz. He and Berlioz had a number of common interests. One of them was the theatre. In 1827, Delacroix was impressed by a certain English actress. He wrote about "a Miss Smithson who has won all hearts."[9] This was of course the same woman who made such an impression on Berlioz.

Eugene Delacroix

By that time, he had already begun to make his mark in the Paris art scene. Born in 1798, he began formal art studies when he was about 17. His first major work appeared in 1824. Entitled *The Massacre at Chios*, it dramatically depicted the slaughter of thousands of unarmed Greeks during their revolt against their Turkish rulers and revealed his commitment to liberty and freedom.

Wounded Lioness by Delacroix

His most famous work is "Liberty Leading the People," which he painted six years later. It depicts the uprising which resulted in Louis-Philippe becoming king, which at the time was regarded as a victory for democratic ideals. Even though he hadn't done any actual fighting, he painted himself in the foreground carrying a rifle. The French government purchased the painting but never displayed it because it was considered too radical.

He made a trip to North Africa in 1832. This trip had a great effect on his work, both in exotic subjects and his use of dynamic energy and vibrant colors, which greatly influenced a number of painters who came after him. He was very successful during his life, receiving many honors and commissions for large murals and expansive ceiling panels in government buildings in addition to his paintings on canvas.

Selected Works

Symphonic Music
Symphonie fantastique
Symphonie funèbre et triomphale
Hungarian (Rakoczy) March
Harold en Italie
Roméo et Juliette

Overtures
Le Corsaire
Le Carnaval Romain (Roman Carnival)
Le Roi Lear (King Lear)
Rob Roy
Waverly

Choral Works
Te Deum
Requiem
La Damnation de Faust
L'Enfance du Christ
"La Marseillaise" (arrangement)

Operas
Béatrice et Bénédict
Benvenuto Cellini
Les Troyens

Timeline in History

1770 Composer Ludwig van Beethoven is born.

1776 Thirteen American colonies declare their independence from Great Britain.

1789 The French Revolution begins.

1803 United States nearly doubles in size with Louisiana Purchase.

1804 Napoléon Bonaparte proclaims himself emperor of France.

1809 Composer Felix Mendelssohn is born; composer Franz Joseph Haydn dies.

1813 Composers Richard Wagner and Giuseppe Verdi are born.

1814 After Fort McHenry in Baltimore withstands British attack, Francis Scott Key writes "The Star-Spangled Banner."

1815 Napoléon loses battle of Waterloo and is exiled to Atlantic Ocean island of St. Helena.

1821 Napoléon dies.

1826 French artist Joseph-Nicéphore Niepce takes world's first photograph, which requires an eight-hour exposure.

1827 Beethoven dies.

1830 Uprising in France replaces Charles X with "Citizen King" Louis-Philippe.

1832 Charles Carroll, the final surviving signer of the Declaration of Independence, dies.

1836 Mexican troops win battle of the Alamo; Texas declares independence from Mexico after winning battle of San Jacinto several weeks later.

1837 Victoria becomes queen of England and rules until 1901.

1844 Alexandre Dumas publishes *The Count of Monte Cristo* and *The Three Musketeers.*

1848 Mexican-American war ends as Arizona, California, Nevada, New Mexico, Texas, Utah, and parts of Colorado and Wyoming are added to U.S. territory.

1857 The first U.S. baseball league, the National Association of Baseball Clubs, is formed.

1859 French circus performer Charles Blondin crosses Niagara Falls on a tightrope.

1861 U.S. Civil War begins.

1862 Outnumbered Mexican troops defeat invading French army on May 5.

1865 Civil War ends; president Abraham Lincoln is assassinated.

1869 Suez Canal opens.

1879 "La Marseillaise" becomes the French national anthem.

Chronology

1803	Born on December 11 in French village of La Côte-Saint-André
1815	Is smitten by Estelle Duboeuf
1817	Formal musical instruction begins
1821	Begins full-time medical studies in Paris
1824	Earns bachelor's degree
1826	Enters Paris Conservatory as student
1827	Sees Harriet Smithson perform in Shakespeare's *Hamlet*
1830	*Symphonie fantastique* premieres; becomes engaged to Camille Moke
1831	Leaves for Rome; Camille breaks off engagement
1832	Returns to Paris; meets Harriet Smithson
1833	Marries Harriet Smithson
1834	Son, Louis, is born
1839	Becomes librarian at Paris Conservatory
1842	Separates from Harriet; meets Marie Recio
1848	Father dies
1849	Becomes president and conductor-in-chief of Société Philharmonique
1854	Harriet dies; marries Marie Recio
1862	Marie dies
1864	Meets Estelle Duboeuf, now widowed, and tells her of his earlier passion
1865	Publishes *Mémoires*
1867	Son Louis dies
1869	Dies in Paris on March 8
2003	Celebrations of 200th anniversary of birth include those in Singapore, China, France, and the United States

Glossary

callous (CAH-lus)—feeling no emotion for others; uncaring.

cretin (CREE-tin)—an especially stupid or insensitive person.

dissect (die-SEKT)—to cut apart for scientific study.

franc (FRANK)—a unit of French money.

masonry (MAY-sun-ree)—building with mineral products such as stones or bricks held together with mortar or cement.

morgue (MORG)—a place where dead bodies are kept until they can be released for burial or other form of disposal.

opera (AH-p'rah)—a drama set to music, with all or most of the dialogue sung.

quagmire (KWAG-mire)—a muddy or marshy area.

scaffold (SKA-fuld)—an elevated platform used for the execution of criminals.

score (SKOR)—the written form of a musical composition.

symphony (SIM-foe-nee)—a large-scale musical composition for full orchestra, usually consisting of four movements.

travails (trah-VALES)—difficult tasks, efforts, or torments.

vertebrae (VUR-tuh-bray)—bones that compose the spinal column.

Chapter Notes

Chapter 2   First Love

1. D. Kern Holoman, *Berlioz* (Cambridge, MA: Harvard University Press, 1989), p. 8.
2. Ibid., p. 11.
3. Robert Clarson-Leach, *Berlioz: His Life and Times* (New York: Hippocrene Books, 1983), p. 15.
4. Ibid., p. 16.
5. Jacques Barzun, *Berlioz and His Century* (New York: Meridian Books, 1956), p. 35.

Chapter 3   Musician or Physician?

1. D. Kern Holoman, *Berlioz* (Cambridge, MA: Harvard University Press, 1989), p. 17.
2. Hugh Macdonald, *Berlioz* (London: J. M. Dent Ltd., 1982), p. 5.
3. Harold Schonberg, *The Lives of the Great Composers* (New York: W. W. Norton, 1981), p. 155.
4. Ibid., p. 157.
5. Macdonald, *Berlioz*, p. 6.
6. Ibid., p. 13.
7. Ibid., pp. 13–14.
8. Ibid., p. 18.
9. Robert Clarson-Leach, *Berlioz: His Life and Times* (New York: Hippocrene Books, 1983), p. 49.

Chapter 4   The Grand Passion Returns

1. Robert Clarson-Leach, *Berlioz: His Life and Times* (New York: Hippocrene Books, 1983), p. 58.

Chapter 5   Reality Strikes

1. D. Kern Holoman, *Berlioz* (Cambridge, MA: Harvard University Press, 1989), p. 173.
2. Ibid.
3. Harold Schonberg, *The Lives of the Great Composers* (New York: W. W. Norton, 1981), p. 165.
4. Peter Bloom, *The Life of Berlioz* (Cambridge, England: Cambridge University Press, 1998), p. 102.
5. Stanley Sadie, editor, *The New Grove Dictionary of Music and Musicians,* Volume 2 (London: Macmillan Publishers Ltd., 1980), p. 586.

Chapter 6   Final Troubles

1. Robert Clarson-Leach, *Berlioz: His Life and Times* (New York: Hippocrene Books, 1983), pp. 88–89.
2. Peter Bloom, *The Life of Berlioz* (Cambridge, England: Cambridge University Press, 1998), pp. 156–57.
3. Hugh Macdonald, *Berlioz* (London: J. M. Dent Ltd., 1982), p. 65.
4. Ibid., p. 66.
5. Bloom, *The Life of Berlioz*, p. 174.
6. Macdonald, *Berlioz*, p. 68.
7. Ibid., p. 69.
8. Bloom, *The Life of Berlioz*, p. 176.
9. Art; http://www.uaf.edu/english/faculty/reilly/NCHCproject/Art.htm
Eugene Delacroix, 1798-1863, France
http://www.nelepets.com/art/artists/d/Delacroix-bio.htm

For Further Reading

For Young Adults

Jacobson, Julius. *The Classical Music Experience*. Naperville, IL: Sourcebooks, Inc., 2003.

Wasselin, Christian. *Berlioz—First Discovery Music*. Translated by Penelope Stanley-Baker. Includes CD. London: ABRSM Publishing, 2003.

Works Consulted

Barzun, Jacques. *Berlioz and His Century*. New York: Meridian Books, 1956.

Bloom, Peter. *The Life of Berlioz*. Cambridge, England: Cambridge University Press, 1998.

Clarson-Leach, Robert. *Berlioz: His Life and Times*. New York: Hippocrene Books, 1983.

Holoman, D. Kern. *Berlioz*. Cambridge, MA: Harvard University Press, 1989.

Macdonald, Hugh. *Berlioz*. London: J. M. Dent Ltd., 1982.

Sadie, Stanley (editor). *The New Grove Dictionary of Music and Musicians*. Volume 2. London: Macmillan Publishers Ltd., 1980.

Schonberg, Harold. *The Lives of the Great Composers*. New York: W. W. Norton, 1981.

On the Internet

The Hector Berlioz Web Site
http://www.hberlioz.com

The Classical Music Archives, "Biography of Hector Berlioz"
http://www.classicalarchives.com/bios/codm/berlioz.html

"La Marseillaise"
http://www.marseillaise.org/english/background.html

A Famous French Writer
The Literature Network, "Alexandre Dumas"
http://www.online-literature.com/dumas/

Smithsonian Magazine, "The Life and Resurrection of Alexandre Dumas," July 1996

http://www.smithsonianmag.si.edu/smithsonian/issues96/jul96/dumas.html

Who Invented Baseball?
Baseball Library, "Abner Doubleday"
http://www.pubdim.net/baseballlibrary/ballplayers/D/Doubleday_Abner.stm

Baseball Library, "Alexander Cartwright"
http://www.pubdim.net/baseballlibrary/ballplayers/C/Cartwright_Alexander.stm

National Baseball Hall of Fame, "The Origins of the National Baseball Hall of Fame and Museum"
http://www.baseballhalloffame.org/about/history.htm

Mr. Baseball, "Baseball History"
http://www.mrbaseball.com/history/doubleday.htm

The Birth of the U.S. National Anthem
"Francis Scott Key"
http://www.usflag.org/francis.scott.key.html

Smithsonian Institution, "Star-Spangled Banner and the War of 1812"
http://www.si.edu/resource/faq/nmah/starflag.htm

Walking a Tightrope
Blithering Antiquity, "Whatever Happened to . . . Blondin?" February 2003
http://www.hornpipe.com/ba/ba2b.htm

Cinco de Mayo
Mexico Connect, "Maximilian and Carlota: The 'Archdupe' and His Tragic Lady," by Jim Tuck, 1999
http://www.mexconnect.com/mex_/history/jtuck/jtmaximilian.html

"Maximilian of Mexico," by Kerry R. J. Tattersall
http://www.austrian-mint.com/e/maxhist.html

"Mexican Holidays: Cinco de Mayo"
http://www.mexonline.com/cinco.htm